The
Xenophobe's Guide to
The Japanese

Sahoko Kaji
Noriko Hama
Jonathan Rice

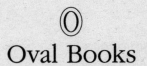

Oval Books

Published by Oval Books
335 Kennington Road
London SE11 4QE
United Kingdom

Telephone: +44 (0)20 7582 7123
Fax: +44 (0)20 7582 1022
E-mail: info@ovalbooks.com
Web site: www.ovalbooks.com

Published by Oval Books, 1999
Reprinted 2000
Updated 2002, 2004

Editor – Catriona Tulloch Scott
Series Editor – Anne Tauté

Cover designer – Jim Wire, Quantum
Printer – Cox & Wyman Ltd.
Producer – Oval Projects Ltd.

Xenophobe's® is a Registered Trademark.

ISBN-13: 978-1-902825-36-5
ISBN-10: 1-902825-36-5

Contents

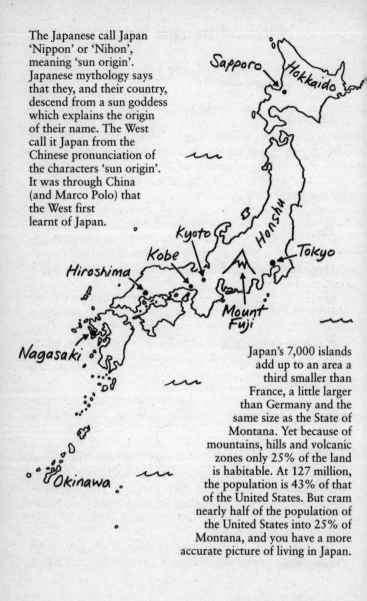

The Japanese call Japan 'Nippon' or 'Nihon', meaning 'sun origin'. Japanese mythology says that they, and their country, descend from a sun goddess which explains the origin of their name. The West call it Japan from the Chinese pronunciation of the characters 'sun origin'. It was through China (and Marco Polo) that the West first learnt of Japan.

Sapporo

Hokkaido

Kyoto

Honshu

Kobe

Tokyo

Hiroshima

Mount Fuji

Nagasaki

Okinawa

Japan's 7,000 islands add up to an area a third smaller than France, a little larger than Germany and the same size as the State of Montana. Yet because of mountains, hills and volcanic zones only 25% of the land is habitable. At 127 million, the population is 43% of that of the United States. But cram nearly half of the population of the United States into 25% of Montana, and you have a more accurate picture of living in Japan.

Nationalism and Identity

The Ins and Outs of Being Japanese

The Japanese do to strangers things they would never do to each other. They do in foreign countries things they would never do at home. This is because there is a stark distinction between what is *uchi* (being on the inside) and what is *soto* (being on the outside). To be taken seriously, to receive proper attention to your well-being, in other words to matter to the Japanese, you must be *uchi*. If you are not, you can expect little consideration: you are *soto*, and what you will get is benign neglect. You are invisible. To the Japanese, foreigners are *soto* most of the time.

Japan is *uchi*, abroad is not, so your behaviour can be different overseas. Nobody at home will hear about it. 'Embarrassment on the road is left behind' as the proverb conveniently goes.

Because Japan is an island country, surrounded by difficult and dangerous seas, the Japanese have remained racially undiluted for many hundreds of years. They consider one of their strengths to be their homogeneity: sentences often begin with the phrase "We Japanese", as though all Japanese act identically and hold exactly the same opinions about every subject.

The geography of Japan has always had a strong influence on the character of its inhabitants. Since records began (about the 6th century A.D.), the population has been great enough to make it impossible to live as a hermit for long. In the 10th century, Kyoto, then the capital of Japan, was a large city, possibly one of the two or three largest in the world at that time. The Japanese have always lived close to each other, so any idea of individuality, of not relying on another person, is well and truly expunged from the psyche.

To your *uchi* friends, you divulge your innermost secrets. With mere acquaintances you stick to talking

5

about the weather. Under no circumstances should the two attitudes be confused. Thus the existence of a stranger in the lift or the corridor is never acknowledged. Doors slam in your face, elbows ram into your side, brief-cases leave marks on your knees and nobody apologises. But once you are their acquaintance, preferably their customer, the red carpet rolls.

The Japanese do not find this sudden switch unnatural. The distinction between *uchi* and *soto* is about cutting the world down to manageable proportions. It is a method of self-preservation. Though they are brought up to care and feel deeply for each other, it is simply not possible to care and feel deeply for everybody at all times, so priorities must be set. What is *uchi* must come first. It is only natural, then, that strangers come last.

The Japanese are gregarious. They cannot live on their own. If you are a go-it-alone kind of person, the *uchi-soto* distinction will not matter so much. But if you need to be part of a group for survival, becoming *uchi* with the wrong kind of people could be disastrous. The ins and outs of being Japanese are not easy.

How They See Others

To the Japanese, all non-Japanese are *gaijin* (foreigners) who are not and can never be the same as they are.

The term 'foreigner complex' crops up frequently in Japan. In this context the foreigner is the typical Westerner of the tall, long-legged, more often than not blond and blue-eyed variety. For ages, in contrast to the West's 'Why can't they be like us?', the Japanese have asked themselves 'Why can't we be like them?' Many will dye their hair brown or wear contact lenses which make their eyes look blue. Some women buy special creams to make their nipples a paler shade of pink. Considered the ultimate in visual desirability, Western models, actors and rock stars are recruited by the media to advertise everything from cars to cough drops. Anything with a Western appearance is regarded as trendy or prestigious. Producers use this fact to sell their products, and new gadgets are introduced as being 'already popular' in Europe or America.

The Japanese love affair with America runs deep. Asked 'What nationality would you like to be if you were to be born again?', 30% of those polled answered 'American'. The English language is present in every nook and cranny of daily life, though always in uniquely Japanised form. After a workout session at the gym, you quaff a can of 'Pocari Sweat' to get your body fluid back into balance. Feeling hungry, you eat in a fast-food restaurant called 'Happy More'. If you are unemployed, you go to your local job centre called 'Hello Work'.

Neighbours on the Asian continent have recently begun to capture the Japanese imagination. Just as the British tend to say they go to Europe for their holidays, so the Japanese treat Asia as somewhere exotic to visit, rather than a whole of which they are a part. But it is becoming the acceptable thing to don Asian-looking clothing, eat continental Asian food and generally immerse oneself in things Asiatic.

Foreign language schools are all the rage. One radio station airs 20-minute language courses twice a day, except Sundays, in English, French, German, Italian, Spanish, Russian, as well as Chinese and Korean.

Because of all the learning, research, reading, studying and visiting, the Japanese think they know the rest of the world far better than any foreigner will ever know them. Hence any foreigner who speaks Japanese and shows appreciation of Japanese culture is immediately dubbed *henna gaijin* (weird foreigner). The nation is convinced that, though foreigners will never know them, if they suffer long enough, they will know the foreigners.

7

How They See Themselves

If you ask how the Japanese see themselves and get an immediate straight answer, you are not speaking to a true Japanese. For why should things be defined if everything is understood without being explained? Clearly defined lines of demarcation are uncalled for. One thing blends subtly into another in the Japanese mind. Explicit definitions are a potential source of discord. Direct questions are frowned on, so are direct answers. The Japanese will seldom answer a question with a straight yes or no. The normal response is *"Ma"* or *"Ma-ma"*, meaning 'sort of', 'rather', or 'more or less'. Therefore being asked to define or explain something, such as what it is to be Japanese, is a confrontation. Many Japanese pass their whole lives without ever once asking themselves this question.

A Japanese business executive once described the difference between the Japanese and Westerners by saying that the Japanese are analogue, while Westerners are digital. An analogue clock can only give the correct information if the big hand, the little hand and the clock face are read together. No one piece of the clock can tell you the time on its own, and, what is more, by looking at the analogue clock, you can see that if it is half past three now, it will be twenty-five to four in five minutes' time. The hand must progress logically and regularly round the clock face for the clock to work.

The Japanese see themselves as parts of the analogue clock, always working in harmony and progressing logically along the course of their lives. A digital clock, on the other hand, tells the time just as precisely, but it gives its information in isolation.

How They Would Like to be Seen

Despite their self-effacing appearance, most Japanese are proud at heart. They would like to be seen as an orderly, hard-working people, capable of meeting expectations – of being well up to every task. But their ideal is to be super-clever in secret. 'The wise hawk hides its claws', as the saying goes. The reverse is the ultimate indignity.

To this end they push themselves in their work, their sport, even their leisure. When the world criticized them for working too hard, they produced television programmes on how to enjoy a leisurely weekend which everyone watched with intensity at the weekends.

For fear of being seen as layabouts, people will not take holidays. In desperation, companies wanting to encourage employees to go on holiday found that the only way they could persuade them to take even a few days a year was to shut down the works completely, condemning tens of thousands of workaholics to miserable 'holidays' racked by withdrawal symptoms.

Character

Mutual Understanding

The Japanese are trained throughout their lives to read each other's minds. This means it is not necessary to have or to express an opinion. In fact for a Japanese woman to be called opinionated is worse than being called ugly. And an exact translation of the word 'opinionated' does not even exist. To call a man 'decisive' is just as bad.

Because preferences are rarely voiced, one has to be a mind-reader in Japan. This can lead to a lot of confusion, since mind-reading can never be infallible. For example, someone might think you want to leave, when in fact you want to stay, and so on. It can also be a costly business. You don't ask people their dietary requirements when you invite them to a meal. That would be too direct. So you have to prepare for every conceivable culinary contingency.

The quintessence of unspoken mutual understanding is to be found in the word *yoroshiku*: 'You have understood what I want you to do. I have understood that you have understood what I want you to do. Therefore I leave it up to you to finish the task and I expect it to be done in the way I want it to be done. And I thank you for understanding me and agreeing to take the trouble to do the task.' All this in four syllables.

The Japanese have also perfected the art of deliberately misunderstanding each other in order not to cause loss of face. On a hot day in Tokyo, a Japanese father out walking with his children asked the local ice-cream seller what were the ingredients of his *Supa-Kureemu*, as portrayed on the outside of his van. The ice-cream seller gave a detailed description of vanilla and strawberry ice-cream and pistachio nuts, all topped with a glazed honey and chocolate sauce. The customer was sold. "I'll have two please." "Sorry, we haven't got any today," replied the ice-cream man.

A European ice-cream seller would have interpreted the question as a clear sign that the customer wanted to buy the *Supa-Kureemu*, and would have replied, "Sorry, we haven't got any," without bothering to describe it. The Japanese, on the other hand, does not want to have to cause loss of face (his own or his customer's) so he opts for the polite way out. He describes the confection in the hope that the customer will decide against it, then he won't have to admit he is out of stock. He knows the real meaning of the question, but he chooses to answer precisely what he is asked. This happens all the time in Japan. If a potentially embarrassing issue can be postponed or avoided altogether, it will be.

Under the Mat, Behind the Words

The Japanese read between the lines, or, to be exact, behind the words. Everyone knows the true state of things, that behind the *tatemae* – the 'official position' or what is expressed in words, is a *honne* – 'true voice', an undefined mass of human emotions reflecting the actual state of affairs. This stays in the background, to be discerned by the discerning. The Japanese will quietly walk away, mentally if not physically, from anyone who fails to recognise this distinction. Furthermore, their way of dealing with something they find unacceptable is by not talking about it: if it isn't acknowledged, then it can be regarded as ceasing to exist.

Things that might hurt people's feelings or cause controversy are better left unsaid, especially when it comes to gaffes made by fellow insiders. Since it is of paramount importance in any aspect of Japanese society to save face, to 'squash a face' is a major offence and must be avoided at all costs. This often turns out to be the motive behind actions which otherwise seem inexplicable, or illegal, like cooking the books to cover someone else's mistake.

Making a clean breast of it is very rarely the preferred option. Letting things out and making them known to outsiders would be a collective shame. So, whatever can be swept under the mat will be – in as thorough and swift a manner as possible.

In former times suicide was an honourable way of making restitution. Nowadays apologies are seen as one of the efficient ways of getting rid of the embarrassing bits of fluff. Now you see it, now you don't. Once a high-ranking company executive bows his head low and resigns, the slate is wiped clean. You stop asking those awkward questions, for it is not done to persist. In this context, apology is not an admission of guilt, but a means whereby one can exonerate oneself and silence one's accusers.

Nothing is quite what it seems in the Kafkaesque world of Japanese ritual. Form and substance may contradict each other entirely. But it does not really matter, so long as people's faces remain intact.

11

Reaching Agreement

In the process of arriving at a decision, appropriate information is transmitted to the appropriate quarters in the appropriate manner. Those who must be consulted will be consulted, those who need convincing will be convinced. This is the art of *nemawashi*. (The same word is used in gardening to describe a method of transplanting something. You first prune the root and wait until little roots sprout from the pruned part. Then you transplant it. *Ne* means 'root'. *Mawashi* literally means 'binding'.)

To succeed in Japanese society, you must know how to do this and do it well. By the time you arrive at a meeting, so much information will have been shared that the outcome is already predicted. It sounds easy, but in practice the process can be quite complex. For a start, you have to know where the right places are for those all-important roots to penetrate. You can do irreparable damage by picking the wrong way to go, and the wrong people to approach. Moreover, it is never easy to pull out the roots once they have been planted. What was supposed to have been a smart move may turn out to be your undoing if the wrong lot have you by the roots.

The sequence in which the *nemawashi* takes place is also crucial. If the right people are approached but in the wrong order, the whole venture is doomed. If you approach the wrong people in the right order, you may find yourself committed to an unholy alliance totally beyond your control. In that eventuality, the original difficulty that required *nemawashi* in the first place would cease to matter much.

One Big Group

In Japanese society, the line between public and private is extremely blurred. Once someone opens up to you, you are wholly a part of them. Your well-being is their business. They are there for you when you need them and when you don't. They will follow you to your grave to see that you are properly buried. Your private address and phone number as well as your marital and parental status are public property. Precisely for this reason, the notion of *enryo* (a respectful distance) is encouraged. You should know when not to intrude.

With no clear lines drawn between public and private, or for that matter between anything at all, there is little room for individualism. This does not mean the Japanese lack diversity. Inhabitants of Kyoto, Osaka and Tokyo, for instance, find each other different. And the language is spoken with very different accents all over the country. Yet they all share the basic expectation of being cared for by, and depending upon, one another.

Everyone is part of some group and the group comes first. Inside this group, everyone has more or less the same understanding and the same attitudes. As the saying goes, 'The nail that sticks up will be hammered down'. The Japanese cannot understand the self-confidence and self-reliance of Westerners, especially the Americans. 'A man's gotta do what a man's gotta do', says John Wayne in countless films. In Japan, a man's gotta do what his peer group gotta do.

Someone to Watch Over You

To live among the Japanese is to experience a constant tidal wave of communication and concern. People are always looking after you. You cannot escape it.

Leave your headlights on in broad daylight and count-less oncoming cars will flash at you to tell you. Lest you feel insecure as you wait for a train, a constant flow of announcements tells you precisely where the train is at the moment, how many seconds it will take to arrive, how crowded it is, how to stand back in order to avert an

13

accident, whether to hurry and get on board or wait until the next one, in which case you might as well get on with reading your paper – always remembering to fold it into a thin strip so that you do not cause obstruction with out-thrust elbows, another thing you are thoughtfully told to avoid.

Once inside the train, the announcements continue: 'Kindly move away from the doors to facilitate the entry and departure of others', 'The next stop is ...', or 'Please do not leave anything behind you when you disembark' as if there was room inside for you to leave anything behind.

All this minding other people's business tends to make the Japanese unable to think for themselves unless they are presented with options. One thing which constantly flummoxes them in restaurants abroad is to be asked what they would like to drink first. How can they know, without being told what to choose from?

Every product you buy, even toilet paper, comes with instructions on how to open the package and what to do when you've done that. Machines come with voluminous manuals which cover every possibility for human error: 'If the light does not go on could it be that you have inadvertently forgotten to plug it in?' Comic cartoon characters illustrate every step, pressing buttons, opening lids and smiling congratulations upon successful completion. At one reception, even before the champagne was opened, the Master of Ceremonies read out instructions on how to enjoy the entertainment and how to leave without forgetting to collect your coat.

One is never quite alone in Japanese society.

Know What You Owe

The Japanese are moved by human frailty. If someone makes a mistake, apologises, and asks for help to remedy the situation, they can expect to be forgiven. They show their appreciation by never forgetting as long as they live that forgiveness and help was given. This is when the beneficiary has *on* towards the benefactor. *On* means 'what one owes'. Once you have *on* towards someone, you had better not forget it – otherwise you will be excluded from society. Japanese society is an ocean of *on* with millions of people bobbing about in it. Everybody owes somebody, and everybody is owed by somebody else.

It is better not to return all your *on* to someone in one go as this could mean you don't care whether your relationship continues or not. But of course, as *on* is not precisely measurable, if you insist that you have not returned all your *on* even after a particularly grand piece of munificence towards your benefactor, then you haven't. In the meantime, your benefactor may create a bigger *on* towards you. Eventually neither of you can keep track of who owes what to whom (or why). But the relationship goes on and on.

Attitudes and Values

Cherishing the Transitory Nature of Things

The Japanese are especially attracted to elusiveness. Fleeting things are beautiful while lasting things are not. Tastes and fashions change like the seasons. Yesterday's truths can be blown away like petals in the wind. The people have centuries of history which they revere, but they are not tied by tradition because that same history embodies flexibility – the beauty of going with the flow, the virtue of not holding a grudge, the wisdom of knowing that everything is temporary.

Japanese literature is filled with the idea of human frailty and the transitory nature of everything. The embodiment of this is the cherry blossom. Every spring, after its exquisite display (a subtle, whitish-pink, never lasting long enough), the flowers drop to the ground. Once the little petals have been neatly and quickly swept away, not a trace is left. The beauty remains only in the mind of the beholder.

The expression 'Let it flow away with water', similar to the Westerner's 'It's water under the bridge', is an almost eager acceptance of change as inevitable. This does not mean that it is any less easy for the Japanese to let go. They are extremely sentimental: the most popular songs, stories and films are those depicting lost love and broken hearts – all the difficulties of letting go. But they accept change because in their heart of hearts they know that nothing should last for ever.

This mind-set works to their advantage. New models are introduced at amazing speed. Open minds and eager attitudes towards innovation, improvement, learning and progress produced the 'Japanese miracle'.

The obsession with what is new applies to the first oysters of the year, the first bamboo shoots, the latest fashion, etc. "Have you had your first *bonito* (a tunny-like fish) yet this year?" is a standard seasonal greeting around the month of May. No self-respecting Japanese gourmet should place himself in a position where he would have to say no.

Elusiveness being the order of the day, these fads never last long, of course. There is always a market for the new model of car, the latest in stereos. Like the global craze for Pokémon characters, everything will be supplanted in this land of transient values.

In the Middle, Somewhat Mobile

Virtually everyone in Japan is middle class. The Japanese like it that way. They dislike extremes. From childhood, they are fed with proverbs and fables that punish excess, and they grow up to feel happy and safe keeping themselves somewhere in the middle. The key is *chu-yo*, moderation.

A survey showed that 91% have *churyu ishiki* – a sense that they are middle class, and of these, 57% see themselves as *chu-no-chu* (middle of the middle). The middle can shift with changing conditions, any time or all the time. Yet the Japanese remain content with the idea, because their instinct is to adjust to the new middle. In any case, it does not occur to them to look for a precise definition of where they are anyway. This explains why, in every aspect of Japanese society, everything suits everyone. As nobody is select, no exclusive offers are geared to the requirements of a certain group. The services catering to their demands are, by definition, uniform and middling. Everybody is included, uniformly, in the middle.

Be *Yasashii*

For all the apparent worship of the way of the warrior, being *yasashii*, which means being gentle, tender, caring, yielding and considerate, is very important in Japan. Asked what a Japanese values most in a potential spouse, both sexes tend to put being *yasashii* at the top of their list of desirable virtues.

The concept is even applied to the inanimate. For instance, a car or shampoo can be *yasashii* to you, to the eye, and to the environment.

The Japanese love of ambiguity has a lot to do with the obsession with *yasashii*. If one is too explicit, one risks being 'hard', which of course is very un-*yasashii*. If you are a very *yasashii* person, you are inclined to leave a lot of things quietly unspoken and gently enigmatic.

The outcome of all this subtlety can be disconcerting. If you get in a lift with other people, as a properly *yasashii* person you obviously have to let the others out first. But it is not correct to tell other people to get out before you, for that would be presumptuous. And as everybody feels the same way, nobody gets out of the lift.

Orderliness

In offices and factories, in classrooms and clinics, signs on the walls urge everyone to keep everything in order. Something that has been taken out and used must go back where it came from. Things that are no longer needed must be properly disposed of. If two things serve one purpose, get rid of one of them.

Documents are expected to be clean, neat and correct. They must also be kept in order so they can be found the moment they are needed, hence the folders with transparent cases, indexes and little stickers to show titles in five different colours. There are also stickers and stamps to indicate which files are out, urgent, secret, and so on.

Order is important at home too, especially in the cities where space is extremely limited. Every square millimetre of the apartment must be employed. Rooms have to be versatile: bedrooms at night and living rooms by day. So the futon bedding is folded neatly away every morning, and clothes must be in cupboards and books on shelves. Even Japanese teenagers have to be tidy.

Partitions and partitioned containers make the most efficient use of your cupboard space. Shelves are narrow enough to fit in between the bookshelf and the television. Chests are available that just fit into that corner; little plastic pockets and baskets are magnetically mounted on your washing machine and fridge.

All these gadgets and arrangements are advertised for their ability to keep your home and office neat and tidy. They help the Japanese satisfy their desire to organise not just themselves, but also their surroundings.

Organisation is not just a personal fetish, it may be essential for survival in a land where earthquakes are a normal event. Lack of organisation in the face of a natural disaster would cause havoc, and the Japanese are not good at havoc. Every family has municipal instructions about what to do if an earthquake should strike. The most conscientious will have a prearranged place to meet if the members of the family are separated – the children at school, the husband at work and the wife at the shops – and a cupboard full of tinned foods and bottled water sufficient to last for a few days if the worst should happen, as it did in Kobe in 1995. Japan is on an earthquake belt, and to have the ground shake under your feet on a regular basis certainly reminds you of the transitoriness of life.

The houses are planned for contingencies too. In the past they were built of wood and ricepaper, with thatched or tiled roofs, and if an earthquake came, they fell over and were built up again. These days they may be large modern blocks of ferro-concrete, but they are designed to stand up to all but the most devastating tremors. The Japanese passion for order derives not just from lack of space in every home but is also the antidote to natural calamity.

Etiquette

Auto-pilot Politeness

The Japanese are polite even when they don't mean to be. It comes with tradition. The language and the culture make it almost impossible to be impolite. When a taxi-driver shouted at another driver who cut in on him, the *gaijin* in his cab asked his Japanese fellow passenger what the expletive used actually meant. The reply showed that even under extreme duress the Japanese retain their politeness: "It means, 'Go to hell, honourably'."

The Japanese culture is supposed to be a non-verbal one in which many things are left subtly unsaid, yet when it comes to auto-pilot politeness, there is much that has to be vocalised before the action can begin.

On sitting down to a meal, you cannot just start eating. You have to announce your intention that you will now begin to avail yourself of the hospitality afforded you ('*Itadakimasu*'). This is not just if you have been invited out to dinner. You say the same at home, even when you yourself have made the meal that everybody is sitting down to. You say it in a restaurant where you have gone with a friend. The chef is clearly out of hearing, and you both pay for your own meal, so who are you being polite to? Never mind, it's all automatic. Nor do you just walk away at the end of the meal. The thing to say then is: "What a delicious treat that was" ('*Gochisosama*') – even if it wasn't. Some would equate this with insincerity, but it's not. It's just politeness without a cause.

Entering someone else's property also has its set of rules. On going into an office, one expresses one's regret for the intrusion ('*Ojama-shimasu*'), even if the meeting is taking place at the other party's request.

"I'm home!" ('*Tadaima*') is not something you shout at a spouse who fails to come to greet you. It's something you say on returning to the office from a conference, or coming home to your mother after school. Similarly, you say "I'm going" ('*Itte kimasu*') even when the action so clearly suits the words that it could not be more superfluous.

Modesty Counts

Japanese modesty takes many forms. In the hot spring resorts, where people sit naked in hot water in the open air, the only sop to modesty is a tiny hand towel, no bigger than a flannel, which has to cover all those parts that prying eyes should not reach. Many people, with only their head above the waterline, chat amiably to passers-by with their tiny towel neatly folded on their head – covering the only part available even if it doesn't need to be covered, as a symbol of their modesty.

Money is another complicated subject for the Japanese. It may be used, but not seen. Since cheques are rarely used and credit cards not yet as common as elsewhere, you have to carry out a lot of transactions in hard cash, but without being seen to do so. If you have borrowed money from somebody, you should not hand 'stark naked' cash back to them. That would be rude. Ideally, the money should be placed in a envelope. Failing that, it should at least be wrapped in something, even tissue paper. And you never thrust well-fingered, wrinkly banknotes at people. You go to the bank first and have them exchanged for the crisp, newly printed variety.

Just to make matters more complicated, money is a very common form of gift. At weddings, funerals and other rites of passage, it is normal for a gift of money to be given. It's no good writing out a cheque or making a credit transfer to the recipient's bank account: you have to withdraw brand new banknotes, put them in an envelope and hand them over. If you wish to do good, it should be done discreetly. Doing nothing is seen as better than doing something and boasting about it.

The Japanese give each other 'worthless' gifts, and introduce each other to their 'stupid' brothers. Comments and actions are constantly accompanied by regrets that one has been 'totally unhelpful'.

The trick is to read between the lines when faced with this sort of thing, or to ignore the lines altogether and focus on the spaces in between. The verbal pyrotechnics of modesty is something that goes with being a sophisticated Japanese person. Civilization as the Japanese know it is measured by how far you can bend over backwards and

21

fold yourself double in grovelling humility, in speech if not in spirit.

"*Sumimasen*", the Japanese for 'excuse me' (literally, 'I am inexcusable'), pops up constantly. In fact, it is often used as a simple 'hello'. It has even come to replace 'thank you' because others are taking trouble for you and you are sorry and grateful for this. The Japanese hear this seemingly all-purpose word countless times a day, from everyone about everything, and *sumimasen* has been almost completely deprived of its meaning. So when true harm has been done and they really want to apologise, they use an expression the equivalent of 'There is no way in which I could excuse or explain myself'.

Set up an appointment with a colleague to complete a task and the first word exchanged is "*Sumimasen*". Enter an apparently empty bakery and you shout it ostensibly to apologise for the inexcusable fact of entering the shop. What you are actually saying is "Hello, is anybody there?", and the underlying implication may well be that you consider the shop attendant inexcusable for not being there to greet you. Double-entendre can go a long way in Japan.

The Bow

Knowing how to bow properly is the sign of a good upbringing and education. Foreigners, being *soto*, are not expected to bow nor indeed to know how, but for the Japanese the bow is a clear indication of the relative status of the two people bowing to each other. The first thing that new entrants to firms, especially in the service sector, are trained in is the proper way to bow. One must learn whether to leave one's hands at the sides or to bring them together in front, when to unbend, and the appropriate degrees of bending.

The long-standing joke about two people never being able to cease bowing because neither may stop before the other may be a cliché. Yet it is not uncommon for pedestrians to be held up while a pair of polite Japanese bob up and down to their mutual satisfaction in the middle of the pavement. In fact, the Japanese naturally learn the timing just as Westerners, when shaking hands, know when to let go.

While bowing is going on, there is not a great deal of eye contact. The Japanese are very wary of direct eye contact under any circumstances. As your head goes down, your greetings, thanks and apologies are for the most part being addressed to the ground. Nor do you have to pay much attention to what the other party is saying. You each express your heartfelt emotions to mother earth, always taking care that your head is closer to it than the other person's. Doing this and listening at the same time is not a feat that many are able to accomplish.

Customers are Gods

The Japanese word for customer is the same as 'guest' or 'the invited' which helps explain their saying, 'Customers are Gods'. Be it in a bank, shop or hotel, if the service provided does not treat them as deities, customers are entitled to express their disatisfaction, and will.

As a customer you will never be hurried. Even minutes before closing, you are invited to take your time and shop to your heart's content and, however long you take, you are bowed out with infinite courtesy and begged to honour the store with your custom again soon. Should you be shopping on a mildly drizzly day, the tannoy will announce: 'Ladies and gentlemen, your kindness in honouring us with your presence in spite of the rain is much appreciated.'

Cost-cutting measures due to the recent recession may give money-off incentives to customers in supermarkets if they bring their own bags, but in department stores traditional pampering is expected. Assistants will neatly fold your newly purchased items, wrap them in layer upon layer of delicate wrapping paper to provide protective covering against potential hazards that the goods may encounter on your journey home. After that, a further layer of more substantial wrapping which bears the store logo is obligatory. A tasteful ribbon in a suitably matching shade will add the all-important finishing touch. The parcel is then placed in a neat and well-fitting carrier bag. (The size of the carrier bag has to be exact. One-size-fits-all is unheard of.) This elaborate packing process is conducted with exquisite precision and lightning speed, after which the assistant will invariably apologise profusely for having made you wait so long.

Punctuality and perseverance are crucial. If a store says it opens at 7 a.m., it will open at that hour come rail strike or typhoon. Home delivery services will come the same day if you ring them to tell them you are now home. Nobody has ever seen an out-of-order vending machine in Japan. When a customer complained of losing a coin under an automatic teller machine, the bank filled the narrow space between the machine and the floor with a little fence.

Quality control is carried to the most elaborate lengths to satisfy Japanese consumers. The most minute of product defects will incur customer wrath. Prompt remedial measures are imperative. Should the manufacturer's name be stamped somewhat askew on the base of a teacup, that would be perceived as a defect. Patterns on a pair of trousers or a skirt have to match at the seams even when those seams lie deeply concealed on the inside of an inconspicuous side pocket. Tolerance thresholds are unlikely to be lowered much beyond the acceptance, when taking delivery of a shiny new car, of one or two specks on the windscreen.

Correspondence

Sending letters involves the Japanese in a lot of protocol. Envelopes have to be addressed just so. If you are a young recruit fresh out of college, you tend to be allotted the job of addressing company envelopes. If you are unable to get the layout correct, you will end up having to do the whole thing all over again.

To omit a title when you address an envelope is considered grossly offensive. There must be one, whether it is Director, Section-Chief or Deputy, *sama* (Mr., Mrs., Ms.), or *sensei* (teacher) – a term preferred by medical doctors and politicians as well as teachers. On the other hand, it is equally outrageous to add a title after your own name. Both practices reflect the idea that the sender sees him- or herself as inferior to the recipient. This is routine, even if you are the president of a company writing to an employee.

When applying for a passport, you are told to submit a self-addressed postcard. On the front everyone writes his or her name without the *sama*. Before sending back the postcards, the passport office diligently stamps the *sama* after each name to make sure nobody receives mail from the government without it. Some 17 million Japanese go overseas each year. All of them have passports. Imagine the trouble saved if the non-crucial practice was dropped altogether. But it is just not done. Thus the passport office workers go on stamping the *sama* after each recipient's name on every postcard. Millions of them.

Table Manners

Eating with the Japanese can be a noisy business. Few are taught to refrain from talking with their mouths full, and some eating sounds during meals are traditional and expected. To smack one's lips is to express satisfaction with what is consumed.

Audible eating can be something of a refined art when it comes to slurping noodles (or tea, unless in ceremony). A genuine Tokyo eastender will do it magnificently, with speed and a crispness of tone that would make any musician envious. Such habits are hard to break, so you might as well get used to them, or learn to tune out. However skilled in the Japanese tongue, no foreigner can be said to have gone truly native unless he has mastered the country's culinary soundbites.

Drinking to Know You

Once alcohol enters the picture, unacceptable behaviour becomes acceptable to the Japanese. The social conventions and the deep commitment to relationships and hierarchy which rule Japanese society are put to one side under the glaze of alcohol. When a Japanese is inebriated, he (and, very occasionally, she) can be his true self. Anything can be, and is, excused, from being sick over the boss's shoes to making gross sexual advances to anybody within groping range, providing the offender turns up bright and breezy at work the next morning.

It is not so long ago that drunkenness was an acceptable defence for any driver who caused an accident. Drivers got off if they could show they were intoxicated, and therefore not responsible for their actions at the time. Nowadays, the force of logic has changed the law so that the legal limit of alcohol in the blood for drivers is zero. Still, left-handedness, which is 'impolite' and therefore trained out of every schoolchild who shows such tendencies, is called in slang 'drunk-handedness', because a left-handed Japanese will only reveal his true inclination when he has had a few too many.

No colleague is a true colleague until a bottle has been shared. By challenging one another's waist-lines with late-night alcohol, and eardrums with out-of-tune *karaoke*, they build up mutual trust. And for this honourable cause society will tolerate anything.

The young are starting to shun this practice. Rowdiness upsets them. They prefer to sit quietly in front of their computers. Still, when they do need to bond, drinking becomes every bit as involved: only in their case, it is more likely strawberry milkshake and camomile tea that does the trick. Even in the increasingly alcohol-free zone of the next generation, bonding Japan-style is a liquid process.

Gift-giving

The Japanese are great gift-givers, especially at the height of summer and the year end. The summer gift season is called *ochugen*, the winter one is *oseibo*. Both individuals and companies become paranoid over who to send gifts to. Christmas and other events are a much more intimate affair. The half-year gifts are one's social obligation, and therefore far more of a headache.

In days of old, people delivered these gifts to each other by turning up unexpectedly on doorsteps and bowing a lot. Now they have them sent via department stores and delivery services to give thanks to professors, teachers, senior colleagues. But it's still a lot of work.

There are a number of criteria that such items have to meet. Since it is more form than content, the gift must not be too personal. It must not imply you know too much about the recipient, nor may it reflect the giver's personality too much, all the more so in the case of corporate executives exchanging gifts for the purpose of public relations. It should be nothing too fancy, nothing too original, nothing too specific. All-purpose usefulness is the thing. So if you stay with the utilitarian, you cannot go wrong: soaps, towels, detergents, dried seaweed, live prawns, preserves, tea, biscuits, noodles, cooking oil, wine, beer, brandy, fruit, vegetables – though not just any fruit or vegetables, they must be rare and they must glisten. (Fruit and vegetables are considered delicacies in Japan, shape, shine and colour being more important than taste. Even an apple is not just something that you bite into casually, but an iridescent object of beauty – glossy red and the size of a small melon, so perfect that it deserves no less than a dish, a knife, a fork, a napkin and seated consumption.)

During the *ochugen* and *oseibo* seasons, entire floors of department stores are cleared for the occasion. Customers wade through the crowds, moving from one display area to another choosing their gifts. In one corner are counters at which you wait in line to be seated, so that you can order this gift to be sent to that household. The wrapping is the key thing. Luckily for the cheapskates, you can buy department store wrapping paper from backstreet dealers, so it's easy to make your gift look more prestigious than it really is. A gift of two kilos of butter wrapped in Mitsukoshi department store paper will be far more prized by the recipient than a gold watch in a paper bag.

The other thing about gifts is that traditionally they are not opened in the presence of the giver. If you take a gift with you to a business meeting and present it with due formality to your opposite number, you can expect it to be put to one side (with profuse and practised words of thanks). Opening a gift in the presence of the giver leaves a Japanese open to the risk of betraying by some slight gesture that this was not the very best gift he had ever received, the one item he still needed to make his life complete. Such a betrayal would cause the giver to lose face, and that can never be allowed.

It is grossly impolite to refuse to accept a gift altogether, however much you may not want yet another tinned ham. The concept of indebtedness means that the Japanese feel an obligation to repay in kind every gift received, and to be safe they will always value a gift they have received slightly higher than its real worth. So there is a very real danger of mutual gift-giving spiralling out of

28

control in a welter of ever more expensive gifts, all perfectly wrapped and rarely opened. To be kinder to one another, it is better not to put someone in your debt in the first place.

Family Matters

Family values are important. Even the company owner likes to be looked on as the father figure, and political factions are likely to refer to their leader as Our Big Dad.

The Japanese family is an institution that has so far held up pretty well. During the period of high economic growth in Japan, every aspect of life had one aim. To catch up with the West. To achieve that end, parents had a role to play. Every Japanese got married and produced offspring, whether they wanted to or not. The father worked and earned, day and night. The mother took care of the finances, fed the family, kept house and made sure the children went to the right schools.

Now that the goal seems to have been more or less achieved, the proper roles of men and women have become an issue. For instance, on Sundays there is now a great deal of social pressure on the husband to take the children on outings to give the wife a break. The eagerness with which husbands undertake this duty is shown by the name it is given – 'family service'.

Divorce is no longer as harmful to promotion as it used to be. The divorce rate is still low, but being divorced does not carry with it the stigma it once did. Younger adults are allowed to make one 'mistake' – it even gives them an aura of worldliness, and divorced families are even appearing in TV dramas, a sign of its growing acceptability.

Because marriages no longer produce heirs at the rate they used to, a great fear is that, at current rates of reproduction, the Japanese population will peak in the year 2007, thereafter to shrink steadily towards nothingness.

There are good reasons for the decision to have fewer, or even no children. For one thing, it is simply too expensive, housing and education costs being what they are. For another, good and affordable nurseries, kindergartens and baby-sitters are in short supply. Child-minding has not even reached infant industry status in Japan.

But the biggest reason is that women's attitudes are changing. Women are still expected to become first and foremost good mothers, but as the number of working mothers increases, they are beginning to rebel against a society which has neglected to share their worries about how to be employees and mothers at the same time. A growing number of men are willing to take childcare leave in their wives' place and to do the chores, but the majority of husbands sit and expect meals to emerge magically from the kitchen.

Some women are not just refusing to have children, they are not getting married in the first place. They are revolting against employers who automatically interpret a woman's marriage as her retirement, and against mothers who brought up a generation of young men who cannot even wash their own underwear.

Senior Citizens

The place of the elderly in the Japanese household is also in peril. As the population ceases to expand and grows old at a faster rate than any other advanced economy, caring for the aged in the home is becoming uphill work. It is not helped by a trend among the elderly to divorce.

The lump sum paid out on retirement offers an escape for many wives who have tolerated their husbands while they were away at work all day and deep into the night. Unable to stand them around, wives soon regard their newly retired husbands as 'wet leaves', which stick to everything and are difficult to clear up – an unwelcome nuisance in their previously orderly lives. So, with the children finally off their hands, they take their share of the money and run.

By the early years of the third millennium, there will be more Japanese in retirement than working, and the fiscal implications of this simple fact are staggering. It is becoming a major issue of public policy, and debates are in progress about a system of subsidies for families who care for their aged at home.

The 'silver generation' is Japan's euphemism for its rapidly greying seniors. The quest goes on for their rightful and workable place in the new-age family. For the time being, a golden solution eludes all.

Treasure Thy Children

Japanese children are a thoroughly pampered species. They are actually referred to as 'treasures from heaven', to be coveted. Fewer and fewer of them descend from above, but once they have arrived, they are as treasured as ever. One of those useful announcements on public transport suggests that adults give up their seats for them.

Parents cosset their offspring, financially as well as psychologically, for what seems like an eternity. Twenty is the age at which one legally becomes an adult, but young adults rarely leave home before they find spouses, and the eldest son may never leave at all, come marriage, parenthood, divorce or whatever else.

To a Western eye, Japanese youths appear immature for their age. This is because children are not encouraged to grow up, at least not until they start work. They live suspended in a state of feel-good mindlessness, which is how it should be. Burying them in well-sheltered hiding places is what you do with treasures.

31

The Various Faces of Japanese Sex

Japanese sexuality has several faces. One is the apparently traditional face of self-righteous reticence. Abstinence is a shared virtue, and marriage is sacred. The percentage of babies born to mothers under 20 is low. Until recently, living together before marriage was not approved. It is still not routine and seldom acknowledged.

Another face is that of vibrant and open pornography. Vending machines dispense an array of adult magazines on every street corner. You can buy them at any time of day or night, without exchanging a word with anyone. Nor is it just 'girlie' magazines that have indecent photographs and stories, and risqué comic strips. Magazines featuring politics and gossip also have them, and erotic novels appear quite casually in leading daily newspapers. *Manga*, a gloriously creative world of adult comic fiction, is often the vehicle for the most imaginative and disturbing displays of Japanese modern-day erotica.

Prostitution is illegal but red-light districts exist. Sheets and sheets of advertisements showing scantily clad young women with their telephone numbers are left in letter boxes of ordinary households every day. More and more high-school girls are entering the sex industry. It is easy for them to do so by using dating clubs, mobile phones and bleepers. They are paid in the form of cash or designer clothing. Sex with high-school girls is in such demand that some older women dress up in school uniform.

The unconsummated relationship, platonic love, is yet another face of Japanese sexuality. Ecstatic purity has always held an attraction for the sentimental Japanese mind. Star-crossed lovers vowing everlasting chastity is what makes Japanese hearts flutter.

The physical side of married love is not simple either. Because married couples live with their children and, often, their parents in tiny apartments with sliding paper doors between rooms, there is not much privacy. So they resort to another haven of anonymous intimacy – the Love Hotel. Love hotels can be found all over Japan: gaudy buildings built to resemble anything from a wedding cake to a cruise liner where rooms can be rented by the hour. For propriety's sake, women will crouch down as low as they can inside the car as they approach the entrance to the Love Hotel, so they will not be spotted, but once inside, nobody acknowledges anybody's existence: disembodied hands collect the money and doors are remote controlled. All guests are definitely *soto*.

Tougher for the Women

Gender discrimination, male chauvinism and sexual harassment are accepted and tolerated. So much social conditioning has gone into making women believe that silence is the better part of wisdom, that it will take several decades of counter-offensive to break the mould.

Foreigners tend to have a fixed view of Japanese women. So do the Japanese. The two are not far apart. Japanese maidens must be mild and meek, swift to hear and slow to speak. Wives must be the embodiment of equanimity, tranquillity and modesty. In fact, nothing could be further from the truth. Japanese women are streetwise and good at coping with crises. Their endurance thresholds are high and they can think laterally. In short, they are tough – but they must not appear so. If they show their true colours, though they may be revered and certainly feared in secret, they are branded as shameless, and consigned to public ridicule.

Thus the new Japanese woman has at the same time to be silent but articulate, diffident but forthright, frail but robust, frivolous but profound, emotional but cool-headed, weepy but ruthless, careful but daredevil, submissive but independent. It's a bit of a tough act to deliver.

Hygiene, Health and Looking Good

Bye bye, Bacteria

The Japanese like to keep things clean, but really clean. Early morning routines for shopkeepers include sweeping the pavement frontage. Convenience store assistants wipe the rubbish bins in front of their shops. Meter-men dust the parking meters and restore them to their original pristine white, before reading them. Airline employees get down on their knees in front of check-in counters with sticky tape in their hands to pick lint off the carpets.

In every home, however small, there is a space near the entrance where outdoor shoes must be taken off and replaced by slippers. 'To come in with their shoes on' is a metaphor for being extremely impolite. There are even special slippers to put on for the lavatory with 'Toilet' written on them.

The Japanese just cannot understand the Western idea of relaxing in soap-scummed bathwater. They soap themselves first, rinse themselves off and then step into the piping hot bath for a deeply satisfying soak.

The love of cleanliness is partly out of necessity. The bulk of the country lies between the latitudes of 30° and 40°, the same latitude as California and Crete. It can get pretty hot and humid during the summer.

Of late their obsession with hygiene seems to have taken something of a giant leap towards the absurd. Bacteria-resistant goods are all the rage – kitchen utensils, cutting-boards, toilet bowls, towels, curtains, ballpoint pens, sheets, socks, toys... It all adds up to a market of 500 billion yen a year.

It is not just possessions that have to be germ-free. Your own person has to be squeaky clean in every respect, and not a hint of physicality must you exude. Young Japanese take pills so that when they emerge from toilet cubicles, they leave not a whiff of tell-tale smell.

They can be so upset if they forget to take this daily dose that they make do without relieving themselves for the entire day.

The mouse attached to the office computer is a possible transmitter of bacteria, unless it too is of the aseptic variety, so you don't grab hold of it directly. You first wrap your own germ-free handkerchief around it, and then and only then are you ready to get on with double clicking.

Insert your anti-bacteria bank card into the automatic teller machine and it feeds you banknotes that have been sterilized somewhere in the dispensing process. Office telephones are regularly sprayed with anti-bacteria spray. Taxi drivers wear white gloves. Nothing is left to chance.

Hello, High-tech in the Cubicle

From simple holes in the ground, most Japanese lavatories have evolved into what now look more like computerised cockpits. Fully equipped, they come with heating devices that keep your rear quarters warm for the duration of your stay, and adjustable nozzles that squirt well-timed and well-aimed water at you from below, followed by a blow-dry.

Such state-of-the-art devices are installed in most Japanese homes these days. As a result, children tend to shy away from the old-fashioned low-tech variety still found in schools, let alone the fossil-age monstrosities above which you have to hover.

The Sound of Silence

Everything that goes on in ladies' lavatories in Japan has to remain discreet. Fearful that sounds would disclose what was happening behind the closed door, Japanese women used to flush while using the toilet. Not to flush per se, but to produce the sound of running water which drowned out the other sounds. Seeing an opportunity to save water and make money at the same time, Japanese manufacturers came up with a little electronic device which many public lavatories (the ladies' at least) now have mounted next to the toilet paper. Press a button and it will play the sound of water being flushed. One such contraption is called affectionately Melody Princess.

Some of these machines have a row of tiny lights which come up one by one, from left to right, to tell you how much longer the recording will last. Press the button again at the appropriate moment, and you are safe to sit back and relax as long as you like behind a reassuringly never-ending sound barrier.

Physical Fitness

Largely due to their diet of fish, seaweed and soyabean curd, the Japanese live long, very long. Life expectancy for a new-born infant in Japan is one of the highest in the world.

Despite the high number of smokers, everyone is acutely health conscious. Body fat has to be measured down to the last decimal point. The amount of excess flesh that you carry about with you is calculated with brutal accuracy. Work-out equipment, dumbbells, massagers come in all shapes, colours and sizes. A compact little machine can take your blood pressure from your index finger in the comfort of your own home. A tiny pedometer to count your paces can be carried in your wallet or handbag, or strapped on the wrist.

Healthy food is fashionable and therefore big business. There is food which enhances your brainpower, or protects you from cancer, or keeps you young. Here, too, a love of fads comes into its own. One year it may be a Chinese curiosity which is an insect in winter and becomes a plant in summer. Another year it is extracts from fish eyeballs, or leaves from a persimmon tree.

But for all their passion for alternative medicine, for acupuncture and moxa cautery, the Japanese also rely a great deal on conventional pills and tablets. In fact, they import two to three times more than they export. Japan's pharmaceutical market is one of the biggest in the world, second only to that of the U.S.A.

A Pain in the Neck

A large number of Japanese people of all generations suffer from stiff necks, backs and shoulders. The best remedy for this is to relax, which is something that the Japanese find singularly difficult to do. So they try everything else – ointments, poultices, electric massage, acupuncture.

Going to hot springs used to be the traditional cure for this ailment, back in those long gone days when the Japanese were not quite so busy. Now, the springs come to you, in small packets of powder. You shake this into your bath tub at home and behold, you can enjoy that special spa feeling without ever leaving the familiar setting of your workaholic life.

Looking Right

Brand (*burando*) names are very important to the Japanese. A *burando* rice costs twice the price of the everyday grain, and it is not unusual to see a 20-year-old university student clad in designer labels from top to toe. Indeed, every self-respecting young Japanese man has at least one *burando* polo-shirt and every woman at least one *burando* (or fake *burando*) handbag. Even the Muji label – a name that means 'No Brand' in Japanese – has become a 'no brand' brand.

Seeking professional help to improve your looks is a big

fad. One reason for this is the 'casual-Friday' syndrome. Someone designated Friday as the day to shed the dark suits everyone wears to work. The idea caught on and spread, as most things do in Japan. Given the choice of what to wear, people were at a loss. Hence the visits by colour analysts to firms and other organisations to reveal such illuminating facts as the difference between the colour you like and the colour you look good in.

Style and make-up consultants are much in demand, increasingly so among men. Across the nation men-only 'aesthetic salons' offer nail polishing, skin improving, hair removing, eyebrow shaping.

Television programmes and fashion magazines are followed ardently for advice on which *burando* is the trend this season. Forget originality and uniqueness. In Japan everybody wants to be different from everybody else in exactly the same way. To stand out without standing out.

Custom and Tradition

Religion

At a recent count, Japan boasted some 106 million Shintoists, 96 million Buddhists, 1.7 million Christians and 11 million followers of other miscellaneous religious orders, all of which adds up to roughly 215 million people – 70% more than the number of the known population. Yet the figures do not lie. In their usual way of not defining things or pinning themselves down, people practise more than one religion, though it could be said that the Japanese are less affected by religion in their daily lives than almost any other nation.

For the contemporary Japanese, religion is not a matter of faith, but of how one adorns the various events in one's life: births, deaths, marriages, school exams, seasonal festivities, growing up, growing old. For each such event, there is a religious form deemed most fitting (or fashionable) that can be selected at will from the vast array of practices at the average Japanese person's disposal. It is religious à-la carte-ism at its most refined.

At birth, you may have been presented at your local Shinto shrine for a blessing. Your umbilical cord may be kept wrapped in highest quality cotton wool and ensconced in a tiny wooden box in the manner of a holy Shinto relic. But that does not stop you having a splendid Buddhist funeral. Nor need you have any qualms about getting married in a picturesque Catholic church. A total absence of biblical knowledge is no deterrent to young Japanese attending Midnight Mass on Christmas Eve on their way to or from a gathering where carols are sung and cherubs adorn a magnificent fir tree. Come the New Year, everyone eats, drinks, and generally makes merry in accordance with rituals and customs rooted in the Shinto tradition, the significance of which has long been forgotten.

Superstition of the 'touch-wood' variety is rife. Don't sleep with your head at the northern end of the bed because that is how the dead are laid out before cremation. The entrance to your home has to be facing the right direction for you, otherwise you are doomed to misery for the rest of your life. Don't marry a person with an incompatible blood group, or a woman born in the year of the Horse. There is a correct day for doing everything. Get married on the wrong day and... Yet all this is treated with an air of frivolity and of keeping up appearances. It's a question of hedging one's bets. Better to be comprehensive than sorry.

New Year

The start of the New Year is magical for the Japanese. It is not just a simple 'out with the old, in with the new'.

Somehow, with the notion of a year switching from old to new, all blunders and sins in the old one are discarded. The process is helped along by the ringing of huge bells around midnight, at temples all over the country. As Buddhism teaches that human beings have 108 worldly desires, the bells are rung slowly, at intervals, 108 times, to erase each one of them.

The days leading up to New Year are traditionally a frenzied time for the Japanese. Firstly, there is the sending of New Year greeting cards: 'Congratulations on the arrival of the New Year. I thank you for everything during the past year and ask for your kind assistance, etc., in the new one.' Around 4.4 billion are sent each year, more than 35 cards for every man, woman and child.

These have to be sent out in good time to a broad spectrum of friends, acquaintances and business associates. If there has been a death in your family, you have to send out non-greeting cards to inform people that, because you are in mourning, you are compelled to refrain this time from paying your customary New Year's respects. Recipients will then know that they must refrain from sending you a New Year's card, for felicitations ill befit a household of sadness. In order not to put people to shame for committing a social faux pas, the mourning announcements have to be sent out well in advance, but not so much so that people will have forgotten by the time they start thinking about New Year cards. That would embarrass them even further. So it's probably best not to die in the final three months of the year, for fear of embarrassing your family and their friends.

Come New Year's Eve, the exemplary Japanese housewife has to do mountains of cooking to last the family for the holiday period when many shops are shut, you cannot send out for anything, and unexpected guests are entitled to drop in to pay their respects.

New Year is special to the Japanese in many other ways. Houses and offices are adorned with ornaments to keep out evil and welcome the god of the New Year. But before you welcome him, you want to sweep away the filth and grime, along with your mistakes. The nation's appetite for cleanliness, already at freakish levels, doubles at the end of December. Windows are wiped and floors are swept in every house and office. Fifteen workers with four-metre-wide mops spend three hours washing and polishing each jumbo jet by hand because 'the result is less clean with a machine'.

Even male members of the household busy themselves turning the house upside down with their New Year's Eve cleaning. Once all is ready, the housewife rushes off to the hairdresser's, which is open throughout this night of all nights. There she will encounter many like herself, each heaving a sigh of relief but also anxious lest something has been left undone.

The ritual of calling on respected elders and senior colleagues during the three-day festivities is steadily going out of fashion, but people still flock to shrines and temples to pray for good fortune throughout the year to come. Praying and offering is done en masse at any time after sunset on 31st December until late on 3rd of January. It does not matter exactly when you go, nor where you go, nor who you pray to. Offerings are made by tossing coins into a huge box or area in front of the temple altar. The act of moving to the front is not that difficult, what with people pushing from behind and police on duty for crowd-control. What is impossible is staying in place. Before you know it, you are being prodded away from the altar, to make room for the hordes of people behind. Some places receive over three million visitors in three days.

The more traditional Japanese return to their home town for New Year. All means of transport are jam-packed. People queue for hours to get tickets for trains filled to 130% capacity, and cars form queues 70 kilometres long on the motorways. The same situation develops around mid-August for *O-Bon* when, according to Buddhist tradition, one must welcome back and hold memorial ceremonies for ancestral spirits. The faithful travel back again to their home towns. Others just take a break. Whatever they do, they are with other people wherever they go, to, from and at their destinations.

Another New Year's custom of great importance is the handing out of cash to your own as well as your relatives' children. The strain on your purse can be quite considerable if you come from a large family. Nephews and nieces descend upon you in smiling expectation, and the going rate has become increasingly inflated over the years, with sums varying from 3,000 yen ($25) to 15,000 yen ($130) in accordance with seniority. Sweet and well-behaved boys and girls often open bank accounts on the strength of their takings.

St Valentine's Day: the Birth of a Tradition

In much the same fashion that they have absorbed Christmas into their festive traditions, the Japanese have taken St. Valentine's Day to heart. But, like many other adopted Western practices, St. Valentine's Day in Japan has acquired a unique life of its own.

Never mind the Saint, chocolates are what this day is all about. Originally it was declared to be the only day of the year when women could disclose their love, without risking their reputations, by giving chocolates to the man of their dreams. Eventually, chocolates had to be given to men they wouldn't even dream of dating; not for politeness, more for *giri* (obligation). These are openly called *giri choco* and are the inexpensive, mass-produced type. For your true love you go to the more elegant and expensive chocolate shops. And you must not forget the Valentine card. Some would-be brides go further and enclose photographs of themselves in rented wedding dresses. The chocolates these accompany are called 'pressure-chocolates'.

For all this effort, the ladies do get something. Some are taken out to dinner or given accessories and designer bags. Others receive – surprise, surprise – chocolates in return. Ingenious Japanese chocolatiers decided that a month later the men would give chocolates to their darlings, only this time the chocolates should be white. Hence 14th March is designated 'white day'.

Businessmen who receive *giri choco* on Valentine's Day in the office get their wives to buy their *giri choco* for the return bout. This is a serious affair: young female workers will spend days judging the gifts and gossiping about whose wife has the best possible taste.

Leisure and Pleasure

The Japanese are not good at having a good time without a purpose. They would rather not do whatever it is, if they have to do it in a leisurely fashion. This is not how they derive their pleasure. Even when on holiday they seek a sense of fulfilment, a sense of achievement. A hitch of any sort causes acute consternation, since it could result in an alteration to their itinerary.

Endurance Sports

Being good at sport is admired in Japan, but being a sportsman entails a lot of self-sacrifice. Schools offer a range of extra-curricular sports – baseball, soccer, basket-ball, tennis, table tennis, swimming, skiing, judo, *karate*, *kendo*. But they are not for enjoyment. They are there to build character, to learn about discipline and obedience. Training is rigorous. Sport hierarchy is very strict. The coach is at the top, the rest are determined by seniority, with the youngest carrying the heaviest equipment and making all the preparations for practice and tournaments.

The sport that epitomises the Japanese psyche is *ekiden*, the long-distance relay race. High-schools, universities and companies have their own *ekiden* teams. The runners suffer pain and exhaustion to reach the point where their team-mates await their turn. The team sash is passed along from one runner to the next, wet with the sweat of effort. It is this that binds them together and is the embodiment of unity among the team. The whole race can take up to five hours to finish. All along the route, crowds gather to wave and cheer. Those who cannot be there watch on television, and everyone finds the *ekiden* moving and inspiring.

This spirit of self-denial and endurance is the reason why Japanese firms eagerly take on graduates who have spent much of their time at university outside the classroom on the playing field. They know how to be polite and how to take orders, qualifications eminently suited to a Japanese corporate warrior in the making.

But things are beginning to change. As Japan faces new challenges, it is having to go in search of creative talent rather than obedient swordsmen. And as the element of regimentation recedes and athletes become increasingly preoccupied with self-fulfilment as opposed to self-denial, Japanese performance at international sports events has begun to show considerable improvement.

The older Japanese play tennis or golf. Well-organised tournaments are held between offices and firms, with gifts for the winners and gifts that the winners must give in return. You can even insure yourself against a 'hole-in-one' for if you have the misfortune to hit one, you must cope with the expense of lavish gift-giving to everyone who hears about it. This is a reflection of the group spirit: you are not supposed to stand out and be lucky on your own. Your 'joy' must be shared.

Whatever sport you play, you must look the part. It's no good borrowing a set of clubs and wearing a pair of gardening trousers to play golf. If you go cycling, you must have the full cycling kit, as worn by the winner of the Tour de France. Skiing involves kitting oneself out like a downhill racer, and a Sunday afternoon game of tennis cannot be undertaken without two or three graphite rackets and the latest style of shorts, shirts and headbands. The investment in any sport is such that few people give up after just a few games, however much they may dislike it: they've spent too much looking good to let the investment go.

Playing Solo

Gregarious as they generally are, there are some things that the Japanese do better on their own. One of these is having fun. Take *karaoke*.

One of the few truly Japanese inventions, *karaoke* ranks fourth on the list of the most popular Japanese leisure activities (the first, second and third being dining out, travel within Japan, and driving). *Kara* means 'empty' in Japanese, and *oke* is an abbreviation for 'orchestra'. Without the singer, the orchestra is empty, which is an excellent reason to grab the microphone and join in. Nobody listens, and you can bask in solitary ecstasy.

Playing computer games is another solitary pleasure. Yet both these activities pale into insignificance when compared with *pachinko*, that supremely solitary pastime. Though some go to the parlours which offer pink love seats in front of machines for enjoyment by two, most play alone. Splendid in their isolation, row upon row of Japanese men and women of every age and description sit virtually motionless in front of these upright pinball machines. Every nerve is focused on the hand that controls the levers. Eyes glazed, faces expressionless, time stands still. This is the most popular leisure activity in

Japan, attracting around a quarter of the population. At present the *pachinko* industry earns around $200 billion a year from its four million machines – a sum greater than Japan's top five car makers combined.

The art lies in identifying which machine gives you the best deal in which parlour at what point in the day. Some believe that the chance of winning is greatest just after opening-time, which explains why people start queuing in front of *pachinko* parlours before 10 a.m. every day. Others believe new machines are more accommodating than old ones, and this theory makes new parlours very popular. Every *pachinko* player has his own formula.

The pressures to be part of a group, to relate to others all the time, are so great that in their free time the Japanese seek out solo activities when they can be on their own, mentally if not physically, and forget about their social obligations for as long as it takes to win a packet of detergent or complete the disco version of '*My Way*'.

My Car

The Japanese's car is his castle. This is more literally true than outside observers may assume, since buying a house is such a breathtakingly expensive business in Japan that people compromise by buying cars instead. The Japanese businessman may live in a tiny rented flat, way out in the middle of nowhere, but if he is the proud owner of the latest thing in BMWs, he is at least a half happy man.

For many years the overwhelming Japanese preference was for white cars, the symbol of purity, the epitome of cleanliness. Tastes have grown more diverse, but the loving care with which cars are kept glitteringly spotless – be they red, black, green, or anything else – lives on. (One of the first things that the Japanese notice when they are travelling abroad is the lamentable condition of people's cars. To the Japanese eye they look unwashed, badly painted and generally neglected. The Japanese heart aches for the poor things.)

Apart from the quality of the vehicle as a means of transport, manufacturers pay minute attention to other needs of the drivers. For instance, a switch is mounted on the side of the driver's seat for gliding it smoothly backwards and forwards. This is especially for female drivers who prefer not to reach down between their legs to grab the metal lever.

The Media

The Japanese are avid television watchers. Some even have small televisions screens mounted in their cars.

Programme quality varies enormously. NHK, the BBC of Japan, suffers from an identity crisis in its attempt to be everything to everybody. The commercial channels vie ferociously to be first among equals with by and large indifferent results. Television advertising is on the whole strikingly imaginative, although not necessarily tasteful.

The Japanese also read a lot of newspapers. Most households have their favourite paper delivered to their doorstep: an average of 1.2 papers per day. There are five major broadsheets, each with its own morning and evening editions. All have something for everyone: letters, poems, serialised novels, articles on art, books, food, music, theatre, sports, fashion, society, economics, politics, world events, skulduggery and scandals. In the cherry blossom season, in April and May, the newspapers even record the daily northward march of the blossoms, to allow people to plan their cherry blossom viewing parties, *hanami*, for exactly the right day. The tabloids and sports dailies are also quite professional, and slightly wicked in this land of overwhelming political correctness. Tabloids are, of course, bought at the newsstand, and after perusal, surreptitiously left on the train.

Travelling Wide

Travelling abroad, particularly to the West, is special for the Japanese. Any such opportunity will be grasped. You can get away from close-knit human relationships and the constant vigilance of home and go to the lands of gorgeous opera houses, famous museums and vast breathing space. Not too much breathing space, though. It is always better to have someone there with you. That way you can enjoy the best of both worlds – adequate support and temporary liberation.

More and more couples get married overseas. Hawaii and Australia top the destination list, and the U.S. and Italy are also popular. Less than 1% of the Japanese are Christian, but it is just so smart to get married in a chapel or a church, especially abroad. It is also economical, for you have an excellent excuse not to invite anyone from your office. Not even your immediate boss.

Another purpose for travel is eating. The Japanese love to eat and drink exotic fare. Magazines and television programmes share the experiences of those who have been away, enticing the rest to follow suit. They tell you in great detail of that very special hidden spot where no Japanese has ever dared to tread. Thus you all end up heading for the same supposedly exotic place.

So off the Japanese go, equipped with the mother of all globe-trotting guides *Chikyu no Arukikata* (How to walk the globe), plus cuttings from magazines such as *Figaro-Japon* which tell them where to stay, where to shop, what to eat and what to see. The Japanese are really fond of manuals.

If you research diligently enough, there is nothing that somebody has not discovered for you already. The 'global standard' of correct roaming is there for you to follow – strictly, unquestioningly, and gratefully. All the research has to be completed prior to departure, or at least on the plane. Once you have arrived at your destination, no time should be wasted in studying literature – you are there to see, to learn, to photograph and, of course, to buy.

When you travel, *giri* obliges you to find and bring back something for your acquaintances. These presents, often edible, are called *omiyage* and are compulsory whether you are travelling at home or abroad. You may only be going for a day trip on business aboard the Shinkansen bullet train, but trolleys will be wheeled down the central aisle of the carriage offering *omiyage* even from those places where the train has not stopped. Rushing through a station at 100 miles an hour is a good enough reason to buy souvenirs for your office colleagues.

What you buy is not so important as the price. Too expensive, and you will be indirectly asking the recipients to buy you something equally expensive when it's their turn to travel. Hence the popularity of mass-produced thingummies among Japanese tourists. They don't worry about whether their purchase of five identical little key-holders or purses will be useful. They just need to show that they have followed the custom without embarrassing anyone, including themselves.

Humour

The Japanese are said not to have a sense of humour. Yet humour of the most delightful and artistic kind is to be found in the traditional world of the *rakugo*. Tellers of *rakugo* tales are the apotheosis of stand-up comedians, or rather, sit-down comedians – for they do their story-telling while seated, kimono-clad, on Japanese-style cushions. Without the aid of anything more than a fan, they transport the audience into a timeless world of strutting samurai, sharp-tongued townsfolk, village idiots and nagging wives. This is a one-man act of remarkable accomplishment. The fan serves now as a pair of chopsticks, now as a decanter of *sake*, now as a lance, now a pen, now a pole from which dangle a street vendor's wares.

The Japanese laugh at this because the performance is real and funny, and because they can associate with the underlying theme of human frailty – the character who is slow on the uptake and ends up being tricked by others, or one who tries to be good but fails, gets into trouble and has to be rescued with the help of a wiser fellow. Their laughter comes from compassion and empathy.

Only by making fools of themselves can the Japanese feel truly comfortable with each other and able to laugh. They expect their fellow insiders to do and feel the same. Hence the television game shows in which ordinary people willingly participate in what seems like self-torture.

Another source of mirth is word-play. For example, the Japanese word for divorce is *rikon*. Divorce has become a trend among young couples returning from honeymoon abroad, caused, they say, by disillusionment on the part of the young bride. Until the couple's departure her husband seemed to be in control, full of confidence and able to protect her. Once outside Japan, however, the bride suddenly sees him as timid, lost and unable even to communicate the most basic needs to a waiter. This is not what she expected. What should she do? Get a *rikon*. So they arrive back at Tokyo Narita airport, and get a '*Narikon*'.

On the whole, however, the Japanese prefer to leave humour to the professionals. They will only rarely tell a joke. If they do, they will begin with the words, "This is a joke", so you know to laugh when they stop speaking. Their risk aversion tends to hold them back from irony, leg-pulling or practical jokes in their personal dealings. Sarcasm simply mortifies them. But catch them at their most relaxed, most secretive, most unceremonious, most tipsy or most beyond caring, and they can be very funny indeed. Closet humorists, all.

Business Practice

In the world of Japanese business practice, the old and the new are locked in a subtle tug of war. Underlying values are clearly changing but the post-war stereotype is still very much alive and kicking. People are conformist, organisations are hierarchical, companies expect loyalty, employees expect jobs for life, seniority is inviolate, collectivity is good and independence is suspect.

Unity's the Thing, Stand or Fall

Collectivity is highly valued in the business of running a business: to do things together and to think the same thoughts. So is meeting others' expectations. Persistence and perseverance. Precision and perfection. No effort is worthwhile unless you give it your all. To be seen to have done your best is the thing that counts. Many Japanese heroes, real and fictional, are people who failed in their stated ends.

Collectivity has to walk hand in hand with hierarchy. Everyone has their place. United the Japanese company may be, but democratic it is not. The chain of command is inviolate. Information travels up and down the line in strict accordance with protocol. You never take short cuts or step on other people's turf. While the use of e-mail is beginning to play havoc with this structure, the mentality that flinches at stepping out of line is still entrenched.

The Japanese would not really care whether they win or lose, so long as they were acting in unison. Aiming for the same goal is of supreme importance. Even if you don't get there, it is more noble to fail together than to stand on your own. To Japanese business people, wallowing in self-pity together should be as agreeable as rejoicing together in victory.

51

Equity in Apprenticeship

In-house training of newly recruited employees is very important – how to greet visitors in the company's accepted way, the art of distributing tea around a business meeting. You are shown the way things are and made aware of the fact that you are at the bottom of the ladder and expected to put up with almost anything. Even university graduates begin in business by taking photocopies for their seniors. Where apprenticeship is concerned, it's strictly equal treatment for the budding 'salaryman' and 'OL' (office lady) in Japan, even if the training is for something you will never engage in as a fully functioning member of staff.

To become a salaryman (a white collar member of a big organisation) has for many years been every male graduate's ambition. For women, becoming an OL is less mentally challenging perhaps, but more frustrating, because even the most gifted and determined knows that she does not have a career, she is merely filling in time between graduation and marriage. She will never become a *madogiwazoku* – a window watcher – somebody who is a long term and unsackable employee, but whose value to the organisation is limited to looking out of the window each day and checking whether the clouds are still in the sky, or the grass is still green. Only men last long enough to become *madogiwazoku*.

Loyalty

Both employers and employees have high expectations of each other's performance. They trust one another and are proud each time their expectations are fulfilled. The same positive tension exists between parts suppliers and manufacturers. Or any two Japanese factions, for that matter.

Loyalty responds to loyalty. A company ensures jobs for life and a steady rise up the corporate ladder. Nothing spectacular happens to you in the process: security is what counts. In return, the Japanese employee offers diligence, self-sacrifice, and long, long hours spent working, drinking, golfing, and *karaoke*-ing, all for the good of the company.

But times are changing, and the Japanese corporate culture of continuity at all costs is slowly giving way to a system where high risk begets high return but equally can lead to a high rate of business failures. *Karoshi* – death from overwork – may not be officially cited as a cause of death on death certificates, but it has become common enough for every company to know it exists and to try to ensure that it does not happen to their staff.

The Japanese executive who broke down at a press conference at which his company announced its decision to file for bankruptcy, felt that he and the company had let down their employees in a way that was not supposed to be possible within the rule-book of Japanese corporate practice. He was perfectly able to keep his emotions in check when talking about the company's responsibilities to the shareholders. But the thought of having put his employees on the dole, the sense of having betrayed their trust, proved too much.

If you take away the job security, how can the company justify its impositions on and intrusion into people's lives? How is your loyalty to be repaid, if the company fails you? These are questions that Japanese management was never supposed to have to answer.

Competition

To the Japanese, competition doesn't mean earning more, but serving better. To this end producers fall over each other to read the minds and satisfy the desires of consumers. There is constant pressure to innovate and improve.

The price matters, of course, but Japanese consumers ask for more: a rice-cooker that finishes cooking at the designated time regardless of the amount of rice and water used; a bath tub that fills itself with water of the required temperature at the required time; a dishwasher small enough to fit into tiny Japanese kitchens; a television screen thin enough to hang on the wall, or neat enough to hang around your neck, and for those who have too many recorded programmes to watch, a video-player that plays up to seven times the normal speed.

They want a lamp that emits light which is *yasashii* to your eyes; a pen which is smoother and hence less likely to cause shoulder-ache; cordless headphones; talking microwaves; mobile telephones that vibrate noiselessly instead of ringing to alert you; and for those with smaller pockets, a device that vibrates whenever your mobile phone vibrates in your briefcase.

There are vacuum cleaners specifically designed to kill mites; remote controls not just for your television and CD player but for the air-conditioner and ceiling lights, and to avoid having seven remote controls scattered about in your living-room, one that collectively handles the remote control of all your other remote controls. That's what the Japanese go for.

Systems

Japan itself is a system. This stems from the 'togetherness' of the nation. As in a big company, the people know each other, understand one another, care about each other and identify with each other so that one person's behaviour reflects on them all. The spread and share of information provides society's lubrication. The objective is to keep the greatest number of people equally happy.

Innocence Not Yet Lost

Japan is one of the safest places in the world. The Japanese enjoy the rare freedom of walking around alone after dark without getting mugged. The most high-profile sports car can be casually parked on the street overnight, complete with radio, navigating system, and probably a computer as well, all in full view. It is not necessary to have half a dozen locks on your front door. It is safe as houses, however careless you might be. Homeless people do not beg. They are Japan's street philosophers. Having turned their backs on all that corporate warriorism and those claustrophobic loyalties, they sit in their cardboard-box dwellings, lost in thought, dreaming sweet dreams.

The crime rate is low not merely because the detection rate is high, but because a far worse deterent than going to jail is the shame of letting down one's group and the fear of resulting rejection by them.

So the police have an easy time of it. For every policeman in Japan there are 472 inhabitants for him to look after, but that doesn't worry him because little ever happens. The rest of the world finds it necessary to retain much larger police forces relative to their population: 252 to 1 in France, 376 to 1 in the U.S., and 380 in the U.K.

Police stations have tiny local outposts (*koban*) housing perhaps a couple of friendly policemen, ever ready to tell you the way (even if they don't know it), and look after stray infants or wandering elderly people. Although their ability to cope with serious crime is very rarely put to the test, what crime there is gets solved. The conviction rate for almost every type of crime is very high, partly because the close-knit communities do not tolerate people who transgress the rules, and partly because the Japanese police are good at persuading those they have arrested to confess.

Their glowing sense of security makes the Japanese extremely careless. They walk around oblivious to the fact that their backpacks are open. They leave their bags on their seats while they help themselves at the salad bar.

They are also very gullible. They retain an innocence that has long been lost in most other countries. As such, they easily fall prey to predatory confidence tricksters they encounter in their travels abroad. The roaming Japanese innocent is every host country's nightmare. Japanese tour conductors are a long-suffering species. With so many unguarded tourists to shepherd around all day, their nerves are constantly under assault, and they become totally exhausted. As a result they, too, tend to leave their belongings around unattended.

Where the Streets Have no Name

Streets in Japan are for the most part nameless. Invite someone to your home and you have to fax a map, or count on your guest's car navigation system which transmits traffic information and directions from satellites. 'Turn right at the convenience store, pass three sets of lights, at the stop sign turn left into a narrow street and carry on until you see a tobacco shop on your right...'

Japanese addresses are given according to which area you happen to live in. To understand this, one must imagine looking at Japan from the air. Roughly speaking, the entire country is divided into prefectures. Within these, the land is divided into smaller lots. Within the lots, there are still smaller divisions. Within these, the land is divided into even smaller sections which are numbered. And within these smallest sections, the buildings are numbered, but not necessarily according to their position. They are often numbered according to their date of construction. This is quite logical, of course. The first house built is number one, the second number two, and so on. This is why every building needs a name and every house conspicuously displays a number plate.

Postmen, newspaper boys and other delivery services

require a great deal of experience to be successful. Reaching a destination by road is a nightmare for everyone, including taxi drivers. At each *koban* there is a huge and detailed map of the neighbourhood, which the policemen show to those who have lost their way.

Where the Streets Make no Sense

So much is crammed into such limited space in Japanese city streets, that the effect is like the pieces in a kaleidoscope. Nothing bears any aesthetic relationship to anything else. Shapes, heights, sizes, colours: all are random, all is chaotic.

Loud-coloured plastic flowers adorn the tops of electricity poles and lampposts in shopping districts. At the foot of these poles equally loud advertisements display apartment houses or dating services. The street lamps themselves have shocking-pink, orange or green shades. Little flags of different nations are strung from one side of the street to the other. Awnings used for cigarette ads compete with rows of vending machines to attract your attention. Come Christmas or Valentine's Day, everything turns bright red.

Another thing that is loud on Japanese streets is the noise. Hot-potato and bread vendors drive around in mini-trucks, their megaphones at full volume. In an election, politicians take over – in mini-buses, waving their white-gloved hands (the electors want clean politicians and the politicians want to be seen to be clean), and penetrating the windows of your apartment and your eardrums with their names and promises.

Local government does not sit back and let the shops have all the fun decorating the streets. It puts up signs and billboards, such as the one which solemnly declares: 'This area is designated as off-limits to burglars.'

Other declarations, directly translated, include, 'Traffic

safety city', 'Non-nuclear peace city', and 'Male and female joint participation city'. Any combination of words related to happiness, children and youth will do.

Education

The Japanese education system churns out young people of great mathematical literacy and technical competence. About 97% of eligible youths went on to high school, and 49% of males and 48% of females went on to university. Yet the classroom in Japan does not inspire creativity. It is a place in which the majority of attendees learn a certain number of facts to achieve a given level of knowledge within a given space of time.

School is Hell

In a society where everyone is supposed to be the same as everyone else, any slight difference can become a reason for persecution, like doing badly in sports or in exams, or having lived abroad with one's family. Bullying (*ijime*) is a nationwide problem in Japan, especially in schools. Pupils vent their frustration by picking on one of their schoolmates and making the unfortunate target the object of verbal abuse and exclusion.

Students who go though this trauma often stop attending school. Assault, taunting, extortion – the list is not pleasant. Abuse can come from teachers too, and may become physical. Victims of bullying at school become *futoko*, that is, they refuse to go to school, and suicide as a result of bullying occours all too often.

Although the reported cases of *ijime* are now down to 22,205 cases for primary, junior and high schools from their peak of 51,544 in 1996, the number of *futoko*, which generally stem from bullying, shows that this is still a serious problem. Since records began to be collected in 1991, *futoko* cases have doubled to close to 140,000.

In their frantic attempt to prevent *ijime*, some schools hand back exam papers without adding up the marks.

Exams are Hell

Getting into university is what all good Japanese children aim for. A university education is compulsory if you mean to get yourself a good job. Once your aim has been established, everything starts to work backwards. To get into a good university, you must go to a good high school. To get into a good high school you need to have been to a good junior high school. A good junior high is only possible if you attended a good junior school. A good junior school spells a good kindergarten. And access to a good kindergarten requires special (and costly) coaching at one of the numerous private institutions (*juku*) that exist for the sole purpose of getting children through their entrance exams.

In fact, as such auxiliary tuition is a must at every level of education if the final goal is to be achieved, there is really nothing auxiliary about it. Children who mean serious business get so far ahead in their extra-curricular alternative schools that they stop bothering to listen in the classroom. It becomes the place where they get on with the homework assigned to them by their *juku*. Or catch up on the sleep that is lost from going to two schools every day.

Should you fail to get into university in spite of all this 24-hour preparation, the alternative school really comes into its own. These institutions run full-time courses for young people intending to sit their university entrance exams again the following year. Or the one after that. The *juku* is where you belong while you try again (and again) for the real thing.

University is Limbo

The repeated attempts are well worth it, for once you finally get to university, hell is no more. Japanese universities are there to reward you for all the sweat and tears that have gone before. Their exams are a formality. The production of reports is required more for form than content. You can spend your entire time playing tennis and still get a degree.

Portable phones in their hands, students run from one fun activity to another, sport, music, art, theatre, study-groups, little jobs on the side. The friends you make in this academic leisure-land often last a lifetime, and the romances which blossom into marriage often last as long.

But it is not quite paradise. In reality university is but a limbo where you await your launch into the world of adult Japan. If you get your trajectory wrong, it could be straight back down into hell again.

Government

The present Japanese Constitution was worked out in 1947 under American auspices. Under its provisions, the emperor is 'the symbol of state' but derives his position 'from the will of the people with whom resides sovereign power'.

Parliament, the Diet, consists of a House of Representatives and a House of Councillors. For much of the post-war era the Liberal Democratic Party (LDP) dominated Japanese politics with a predictably persistent outright majority. To all intents and purposes, the political arena was a place of one-party dominance.

The Liberal Democratic Party is said to resemble the Holy Roman Empire. It was neither holy, Roman nor an empire, and the LDP is neither liberal (it is right wing), democratic (it is ruled by a shadowy elite within the smoke-filled rooms of political dealings), nor a party, being originally formed of two parties, the Liberals and the Democrats, and now consisting of a loose alliance of five or six warring factions.

The situation underwent a dramatic change when the LDP were thrown into opposition in 1993. They subsequently got back into power, but Japanese politics continues to be in a state of flux. Parties form, dissolve, merge and separate at the drop of a hat. They are running out of names to call themselves.

For all the dominance of the LDP, continuity has never been a feature of Japanese political progression, even in the years prior to the current state of melting pot chaos. In the period between 1945 and 2004 Japan has had 30 prime ministers with an average term of just under 2 years. This speaks volumes for the nature of Japanese politics, where the attainment of the premiership means little more than that the prime minister is the first among many equals this time round in a rotating system of power sharing. As with everything in Japan, the group is all powerful, but the individual is weak.

Language

The Japanese language is rated as the world's hardest to master. This is probably true for the Japanese themselves, as much as for anybody else. One problem is the various forms of speech that are used to sound polite, respectful and formal. The three are closely interconnected but by no means the same thing.

Written Japanese and spoken Japanese also differ quite considerably, especially in business. If you spoke as you wrote in business correspondence, you would risk being thought of as someone who has time-travelled from the 19th century. On the other hand, if you wrote business letters in the kind of language you use to talk to long-standing colleagues, you would not be far from having to draft a letter of resignation – in the correct form of language, of course.

Although there are such distinctions in other languages, what makes Japanese so daunting is that there is almost an entire vocabulary for each of the polite, respectful, formal and informal manners of speech. But once you have mastered the different vocabularies, your linguistic life can become quite simple. You will know precisely, for instance, how to encourage your guests, in the appropriate way, 'to eat'. And with the proper wording and seasonal greetings at your fingertips, you will not have to worry about how to start off a business letter.

Foreigners learning colloquial Japanese should beware of the differences between male and female Japanese. Many a foreign man has attracted ridicule because his Japanese, though fluent, has been learnt from a Japanese girlfriend. For a foreign woman using the same learning methods to use male Japanese expressions would be even more disastrous.

Just as there are many different ways of expressing the same thing, the same expression can be used to say many different things. The word 'domo' serves as shorthand for 'thank you', 'hello there', 'well done', 'long time no see', 'ever so sorry', 'well well', etc. And there is no way of saying 'yes' or 'no', at least not in the way the words are understood in the West. 'Hai', most usually translated as 'yes', actually means, 'I heard you and I understood you, and I am now thinking of my response'. Too often it is taken by non-Japanese to mean 'yes' when in fact the implication is exactly the opposite.

There are ways of saying a simple 'no' when it would not cause offence to turn something down. But the

Japanese know when they mean 'no', even if they don't say it. "I'll think about it" (*Kangaete okimasu*) is one way of saying a very firm no, and if a Japanese sucks in air between clenched teeth, and then releases it all with a long sighing, "*Saaaaaaa...*", it's back to the drawing board.

Then there is the written language. The Japanese language did not have any writing system at all until Buddhist monks came over from China in the 6th century AD, bringing holy scriptures with them. Unfortunately for all concerned, the Chinese ideographic system, uniquely suited to the uninflected Chinese language, very quickly proved to be utterly hopeless for writing Japanese. So the logical answer was for the court nobles to start speaking Chinese, so that what they spoke could also be written down. But this did not quite work, and over the next few centuries, Japanese evolved as a hybrid language, with almost every Chinese character having at least two different pronunciations, according to whether the context makes it appropriate to use the Chinese reading or the Japanese one.

To read and write Japanese with fluency you have to know your way around the Chinese characters (*kanji*) used in the language (a minimum of 2,000: educated Japanese will know between 5,000 and 8,000 different characters – some of which are made up of over 30 brushstrokes), plus two sets of Japanese phonetic symbols (*hiragana* and *katakana*), one for depicting things ethnically Japanese, another for use in referring to imported things and foreign people's names. But this is much too simplistic a definition of the hybrid phonetic and pictographic Japanese written language. The possibilities are endless, and the pitfalls omnipresent.

19th-century missionaries to Japan apparently believed the language to be the devil's invention for preventing them from doing their work. Modern-day students of the language, whether Japanese or foreign, may or may not believe in the devil, but often feel the same way.

The Authors

Sahoko Kaji is a much travelled economist and university professor. When at home, she enjoys the genial nature of the people and the fact that things work. When abroad, she revels in Western emancipation and independence but constantly finds herself checking that the taxi will indeed be coming to take her to the airport.

Apart from this typically Japanese desire for precision, she has been influenced by the cultures of both East and West for so long that she has accepted she belongs to neither and simply floats somewhere in the middle.

Noriko Hama works for a Japanese multinational. An economist and author with a special interest in economic developments in Europe, she lived in Britain from the age of 8 to 12, after which she was plunged back into the Japanese education system. In the 1990s her job returned her to London for a further 8 years.

She is frequently invited by television and radio to give her views on European and Far Eastern economic affairs which she attributes to her belief that to achieve recognition in her profession you have to be convinced that you are right and that everyone else is wrong. She works hard to give this impression.

Jonathan Rice is a management consultant who specialises in explaining Japanese business style and tactics to Europeans, and vice versa. Since his schooldays in Tokyo, his involvement with Japan has included climbing Mount Fuji, heading a British electronics company, judging the Yamaha World Popular Song Contest, and being Japan's leading bowler in the 1972 cricket season. He loves noodles and *hanami* but can live without Japanese electioneering and *tamagotchi*.